Magical Library Lessons

Lynne Farrell Stover

UpstartBooks

Fort Atkinson, Wisconsin

With heartfelt gratitude to my parents, Bonnie and Ray, for their unconditional support, my "guys" Ronald and Michael for the new computer and technical expertise and brothers, Kirk and Scott, for their encouragement and applause.

Published by UpstartBooks
W5527 Highway 106
P.O. Box 800
Fort Atkinson, Wisconsin 53538-0800
1-800-448-4887

© Lynne Farrell Stover, 2003
Cover design: Debra Neu Sletten

The paper used in this publication meets the minimum requirements of American National Standard for Information Science — Permanence of Paper for Printed Library Material. ANSI/NISO Z39.48-1992.

Contents

Introduction

If, as the saying goes, books are magic, then librarians and reading teachers should be eager to demonstrate this by conjuring up a few enchanting library lessons. Using the works of wonderfully imaginative and extremely popular authors such as J. K. Rowling, Brian Jacques and Lemony Snicket as hooks to catch the attention of students may be a trick, but it is one that works well. Educators thank these authors, who are three among many, for writing about strong characters who use books, reading and research as tools for problem solving.

The appreciation of librarians for J. K. Rowling's Harry Potter books is easily understood. Consider that the library at the imaginary Hogwarts School for Witchcraft and Wizardry is a wonderfully massive room where Madame Irma Pince, the librarian, rules with a firm hand. This ever-interesting place is filled with ancient tomes resting on shelves waiting to reveal the right piece of information that will save the day for our heroes Harry Potter, Ron Weasley and, especially, bookworm Hermione Granger. Intrigue, clandestine meetings and some romance also take place in the library making it the "in" place to be, much to the delight of Muggle, or non-magical, librarians around the world.

Reading teachers embrace the works of Brian Jacques for the imagery, characterization and rich vocabulary found in his Redwall series. The main characters may be talking mice, but they are brave, clever and eager learners. In Redwall Abbey one can find the wise Methuselah recording the events of the day for reference in the future. Solving riddles is as much a part of the drama for Matthias the Mouse in Mossflower Wood as it was years ago for J. R. R. Tolkien's Bilbo Baggins the Hobbit in Gollum's cave.

Teachers of reluctant readers have found a hero in Lemony Snicket. They have discovered that students who often dislike reading delight in the misery and misfortune of the three Baudelaire orphans. In his Series of Unfortunate Events books, the characters may be three of the unluckiest children imaginable, but they are survivors. Using intelligence, inventiveness and the occasional reference book, they always outwit their tormentor.

The authors referenced in the lessons use words, books and libraries to enrich their stories. In turn, the lessons use their stories to reinforce the importance of library skills, research techniques and literary concepts.

How To Use This Book

Considerations Concerning Teaching the Lessons

The 15 lessons in this book were developed for instruction in a library setting during an upper elementary and middle school language arts block. Appropriate for students in grades 4–8, these lessons can be adapted for younger or older students. The lessons need not be taught in sequence, as each one stands alone. With a few exceptions, when it might be necessary for a teacher to continue the activity in the classroom, the lessons can be taught in a 30–45 minute time frame.

Each lesson begins with a quote. These were added to provide a link between the lesson and the literature and are for the teacher's edification. They may be shared with the students to set the tone, but they have not been incorporated within the lesson itself.

The lessons include visuals and activity sheets. The visuals are designated with an eye icon 👁 and are designed so that they can be made into transparencies and used with an overhead projector. However, you can also copy the information onto a chalkboard or chart paper. The activity sheets are designated with a pencil icon ✏. They serve several purposes. If the activity is a student worksheet, you will need to photocopy the worksheet prior to class time. If the activity is a game, preparation time prior to the lesson will also be required.

Each lesson contains an evaluation and extension. The evaluation is usually subjective. The purpose of it is to give the teacher an idea how well the students have mastered the concept taught. The extension could also be considered enrichment. Whereas the lessons can be taught to an entire class, the extensions are usually for a smaller group of students who have the time and desire to go beyond the standard lesson.

Of note is the fact that not every student has read (or is allowed to read) the fantasy book associated with each lesson. This was considered when the lessons were written and it is not necessary to have read the books to successfully complete the activities. There are also built in "loopholes" for students who feel uncomfortable with the monsters and magic that are such a part of these books.

Books Are Magic
Parts of a Book

*A loud ripping noise rent the air: two of the Monster Books had seized a
third and were pulling it apart.*
Harry Potter and the Prisoner of Azkaban

Harry Potter and the Prisoner of Azkaban
Quidditch Through the Ages
by J. K. Rowling

Story Synopses

Harry Potter, a young wizard, is now in his third
year at Hogwarts School for Witchcraft and
Wizardry in J. K. Rowling's *Harry Potter and the
Prisoner of Azkaban*. During this incredibly event-
ful year he and his friends, Ron Weasley and
Hermione Granger, will discover that things are
not always as they first appear. The plot thickens
with revelations concerning the new Defense
Against the Dark Arts teacher and Hermione's
ability to be two places at once. The story climax-
es as an escaped prisoner becomes a beloved ally
and Ron's longtime pet rat is revealed to be the
true villain.

Quidditch Through the Ages is a book chronicling
the history and instructions for playing the most
popular sport in the wizard world. It was written
by J. K. Rowling in 2001 under the pseudonym
Kennilworthy Whisp and has the appearance of
a book that could be found on the shelves of the
library at Hogwarts.

Introduction

In the magical world of Hogwarts, Hogsmeade
and Diagon Alley, books often have unique characteristics. Here books may yell at you or the
illustrations in them may move. In some cases, it
is even necessary to confine aggressive books so
that they will not harm themselves or others. In
the Muggle, or non-magical, world books are
more predictable. However, they are still magic.
It is through our books that we are able to find
obscure facts and enjoy imaginary realms full of
unusual characters.

Time Required 30–40 minutes

Objectives

- The students will review the parts of a book.
- The students will complete an assessment
  and write a book review.

Materials

- A nonfiction book for each student, a textbook (social studies texts work well) or individual copies of *Quidditch Through the Ages* by Kennilworthy Whisp, a.k.a. J. K. Rowling.

- visuals from pages 11 and 12

- activity from page 13

- pencils

Procedure

1. Prior to the lesson, create a bulletin board using the visuals. Start by copying the definition couplets on colorful paper. You might also "disassemble" a discarded book and use it for visual examples of the terms. Assemble the definitions with arrows pointing toward the examples under the title, Parts of a Book, and a quick curriculum-supporting bulletin board has been produced.

2. Decide what books you would like the students to use for the lesson. (A nonfiction book of the student's choice is the most creative, however the students' answers will vary. The use of a textbook is very democratic and appreciated by the classroom teacher. If there are multiple copies of *Quidditch Through the Ages* by Kennilworthy Whisp, a.k.a. J. K. Rowling, using this book is the most fun.)

3. Inform the students that while the books in the school are not as unique as the ones in the library at Hogwarts, they are still magic. This is because they reveal important information to the reader with just one quick inspection. Tell the students that once they know where to look they will be able to find out where and when a book was published, who wrote it and what information is in it.

4. Display the visuals from pages 11 and 12 at the beginning of the lesson. Read the descriptions with the students. (If a transparency is used in place of a bulletin board, it is helpful to use a book to demonstrate these terms.)

5. Give students copies of the activity. Have them work independently or in groups.

Evaluation

The activity sheet may be used for evaluation. If the students have used the same book to complete the assignment, it can be checked as a group. If students have used different books, they may exchange papers and books and check each other's work. (This is an excellent method for reinforcing the lesson.)

Extension

If *Quidditch Through the Ages* is the text of choice, a discussion concerning pseudonyms would be interesting. Tell the students that J. K. Rowling wrote this inexpensive paperback under the fictitious name Kennilworthy Whisp. The book was written as if it were a nonfiction sports history book found on the shelves of the Hogwarts library. (It, along with its counterpart, *Fantastic Beasts & Where to Find Them*, was published in 2001 with the intention that the profits go to charity.)

Ask the students if they are aware of other authors who use pseudonyms for their written work. (Dr. Seuss, a.k.a. Theodore Geisel, and Mark Twain, a.k.a. Samuel Clemens, are two that the students will recognize.)

Ask the students why an author might choose to use a pseudonym. Possible answers:

- An author may not want others to know he or she is writing something. Ben Franklin's *Poor Richard's Almanac* comes to mind.

- An author may want a humorous name. Lemony Snicket, author of the Series of Unfortunate Events books, picked his pen name as a joke.

- An author may want a shorter name. The author Avi is an example.

Books Are Magic
Parts of a Book

~ Cover ~

Don't judge a book by its cover they often say
Though we won't pick it up if it's dingy and gray.

~ Spine ~

A book's "call number" may be small by design
But we are sure to find it on the bottom of its spine.

~ Title Page ~

Title, author, illustrator and publisher
Here all these things we will find for sure.

~ Copyright Page ~

Behind the title page is where the copyright is located
The year a book is published needs to be dated.

~ Dedication ~

Who does the author appreciate and adore?
This is what the dedication page is for.

~ Preface ~

Sometimes referred to as the foreword or introduction
This is an explanation of where the author received instruction.

Books Are Magic

Parts of a Book

Table of Contents

A list of titles of the chapters, topics or sections in a book
It would be a good thing to give this section a look.

Body

This is the largest part, the text's main section.
It is probably the reason you made this book your selection.

Appendix

This is a segment that can be supplemental
With charts, tables, maps and graphs that can be very helpful.

Bibliography

A list of books that were used to research every fact
Will be cited in the book toward the back.

Glossary

If you want to know the meanings of words unique to a book
In the glossary is where a curious person should look.

Index

With the page numbers listed and words alphabetically notated
The subjects found in a book can be easily located.

Books Are Magic
Parts of a Book

Directions: Using a nonfiction book or textbook, answer the questions below.

1. What is the title of the book? _____

2. Who is the author? _____

3. Is there an illustrator? _____   Is there a list of illustrations? _____

4. Is there a preface, foreword or introduction? _____

    If so, who wrote it? _____

5. What is the name of the publisher? _____

6. What is the copyright date? _____

7. How many chapters are listed in the table of contents? _____

8. On what page does the body of the book begin? _____

    What is the last page number in the body of the book? _____

9. Circle the parts of the book included in your text:

    Appendix   **Glossary**   **Index**   **Bibliography**

10. Write a two or three sentence review of the book. (For example, you may write how you liked it, what it looked like and what use it would have.)

    _____

    _____

    _____

    _____

Whatsit, Who and Which
Examining Newspapers

"Please Mrs. Whatsit," Meg asked, "what happens now? Why are we here? What do we do next? Where is Father? When are we going to see him?"
Meg Murry *A Wrinkle in Time*

A Wrinkle in Time
by Madeleine L'Engle

Story Synopsis

This Newbery Award winning book is a classic tale of good vs. evil. Our heroine, Meg Murry, a misfit at school, misses her scientist father who vanished "off the face of the earth." Meg learns her own strength of character as she, her youngest brother, Charles Wallace, and their new friend, Calvin, join forces with three extraterrestrials to save the world.

Introduction

Newspapers inform us on a regular basis the who, what, where, when, why and how in our lives. Like the three "all-knowing" characters, Mrs. Whatsit, Mrs. Who and Mrs. Which, in Madeleine L'Engle's *A Wrinkle in Time,* the role of a newspaper is to educate and entertain.

Time Required 35–45 minutes

Objectives

- The students will be introduced to the various newspapers available in the library.

- The students will discuss the purposes of local, state, national and electronic newspapers.

- The students will complete an activity, simulating the front page of *The Wrinkle Times,* a newspaper that could exist in the world of the Murry children in Madeleine L'Engle's *A Wrinkle in Time.*

Materials

- copies of the newspapers available in the library

- visual from page 16

- activity from page 17

Procedure

1. Collect examples of various kinds of newspapers to show to the students. A good collection would represent local, state and national publications. (A school newsletter could be included.)

2. Discuss with the students the focus and functions of the newspapers available. Point out that each paper has similar features such as news stories, feature stories, editorials, sports reports, information of community interest and advertising. The general rule is, the smaller the newspaper, the more specific to local interests the information contained in the newspaper will be.

3. Inform the students of the newspapers available in the school's library.

4. Display the visual from page 16. Review it with the students. The visual is almost identical to the activity sheet but it has the directions for the activity. (Keep the visual displayed while the students complete the activity.) There are four sections for the students to complete.

   1) Write the date.

   2) Write the beginning of a news story.

   3) Draw a picture.

   4) Write a feature story about "Aunt Beast."

5. Pass out the activity. The students may work on the front page in the library and share their stores and pictures with the class.

Note: If working in collaboration with the classroom teacher, the index may be used to extend the lesson. The students may work in groups to complete the edition of the newspaper, adding comics, crossword puzzles, a weather forecast, etc.

Evaluation

Collect and display some of the students' work near the newspaper section in the library.

Extension

Discuss the following:

1. Will the print newspaper be replaced by electronic news?

2. What are the advantages of electronic news? (It is up-to-date, the paper use is limited, you save money on subscriptions, etc.)

3. What are the disadvantages of electronic news? (You need a computer, you can't read it while eating breakfast, you can't line the bottom of the bird cage with it, etc.)

THE WRINKLE TIMES

Vol. 360 No. 3.14 Planet Earth **1. Write Today's Date**

Children Held Captive on Distant Planet!

2. Create a news story about three young people who, for some reason, are "out of this world." Remember to include the WHO, WHAT, WHERE and WHEN in your report.

See **Captives** Page 4

3. Draw a picture relating to either story.

Aunt Beast Is Wonderful

4. Write a feature story about someone or something by the name of "Aunt Beast," explaining why she is wonderful.

THE WRINKLE TIMES

Vol. 360 No. 3.14   Planet Earth

Children Held Captive on Distant Planet!

See **Captives** Page 4

Aunt Beast Is Wonderful

Profound Proverbs
Using the Thesaurus

"All shall be done ... but it may be harder than you think."
Aslan the Lion *The Lion, the Witch and the Wardrobe*

The Lion, the Witch and the Wardrobe
by C. S. Lewis

Story Synopsis

During World War II's air raids in England, many of London's children were evacuated to the countryside. Four such children are Peter, Susan, Edmund and Lucy Pevensie. Not long after they arrive at the country estate of Professor Digory Kirke, they accidentally enter a wardrobe, an entryway into the magical land of Narnia. Here these Sons of Adam and Daughters of Eve discover that all the creatures living in Narnia are suffering under a spell from the evil White Witch. She has created a land where it is always winter, but never Christmas. One of the children sides with the White Witch, the others with Aslan the Lion. A battle ensues. The children prove their bravery and become Kings and Queens of Narnia. Eventually they return to England through the wardrobe and discover that the professor believes the tale of their adventures and foreshadows future encounters for them in the land of Narnia.

Introduction

C. S. Lewis, author of the Chronicles of Narnia, noted that he wrote these children's books because they were stories he would have liked to have read himself. Born in Belfast, Ireland, he was a scholar, literary critic and professor of Medieval and Renaissance English. His heritage and education contributed to a writing style full of allegory, symbolism and a wonderful command of the English language. Students will enjoy using words, too, as they are encouraged to have fun restating profound "Narnian" proverbs using the thesaurus as a reference tool.

Time Required 30–40 minutes

Objectives

- The students will be introduced to the thesaurus and its uses.

- The students will be able to define what a proverb is.

- The students will find synonyms in a thesaurus to restate proverbs.

- The students will share the restated proverbs with the class.

Materials

- visual from page 20
- activity from page 21
- a thesaurus for each student or group of students
- paper
- pencils
- transparency marker

Procedure

1. Introduce the lesson to the students by explaining that a thesaurus is a book of synonyms. The words inside the thesaurus, like those in a dictionary, are listed in alphabetical order. However, unlike a dictionary, where one looks up words to find meanings, a thesaurus is used when the definition is known but a different, more interesting word is needed. For example, if a character in a story has been described as "smart" too many times, the character becomes uninteresting. A thesaurus will help reveal that clever, bright and brainy are synonyms for smart. (The thesaurus may also disclose that unintelligent, foolish and brainless are antonyms for smart.)

2. Allow a few minutes for the students to become familiar with the format of the thesauri available.

3. Display the visual from page 20. Define "proverb" for the students. Using the visual, create a new proverb with the class. A possible restatement for the proverb "Make new friends but keep the old, one is silver and the other gold" could be "Generate fresh associates but maintain the previously acquired, one is a gray metallic element and the additional is precious yellow bullion."

4. Pass out the activity from page 21. Read over the directions with the class. Allow the students time at the end of the period to share their rewritten proverbs with the class.

Evaluation

The rewritten proverbs will vary according to the ability level of the students. The lesson is very adaptable and has built in differentiation. Gifted students enjoy the verbal challenge. Struggling students and students who speak English as a second language are successful because there are no right or wrong answers.

Extension

The students may create "modern proverbs" that could be published in a book for the library's collection. Some topics for these proverbs could be technology, pop culture and space exploration. For example: "Failure to convert standard measure into metric makes for a failed satellite launch" and "In Sync today, gone tomorrow" would both be modern proverbs.

Profound Proverbs
Using the Thesaurus

A proverb is a short saying expressing a supposed truth or moral lesson.

For example, a common proverb is:

> "Don't count your chickens before they hatch."

This common saying could be restated in a more complex manner. With the help of a thesaurus, it is possible to find other words for *count, chickens, before* and *hatch*. When these words are substituted for the originals, the new proverb becomes:

> "Do not calculate your feathered domesticated animals previous to the time they emerge from their place of origin."

Can you restate this proverb?

> "Make new friends but keep the old,
> one is silver and the other gold."

Profound Proverbs
Using the Thesaurus

A proverb is a short saying expressing a supposed truth or moral lesson.

In the book *The Lion, the Witch and the Wardrobe* by C. S. Lewis, Edmund told Peter and Susan that he had never been to Narnia with Lucy. This was not true. A proverb for this situation could have been:

"Tell a fib you should not, for chances are you will be caught."

In the story, Professor Kirke enjoys impressing others with his knowledge. He might restate the proverb this way:

*"Communicating a false testimonial is not in the foremost interest
of an individual, more than likely the human being in question
will be ensnared in the previously stated falsehood."*

Directions

Choose three of the six proverbs below. Use a thesaurus to rewrite them in a more complex and interesting manner. Share your solutions with the class.

1. "Snow on the ground does not mean that Christmas is around."

2. "A friendly faun is to be trusted before an evil brother."

3. "A lamppost in the middle of the woods may mean many things."

4. "It is dangerous to eat sweet treats offered by beautiful strangers."

5. "A leader can be the Daughter of Eve as well as the King of the Beasts."

6. "Once a King in Narnia, always a King in Narnia."

Magical Manuscripts
The Dewey Decimal System

"Besides, the Latin scrolls in my library need cataloguing, and if I can't find someone who knows a little of the language, I'll have to do it myself."
Kazul the Dragon *Dealing with Dragons*

Dealing with Dragons
by Patricia C. Wrede

Story Synopsis

Kazul the Dragon and Princess Cimorene make a formidable pair. Kazul may be a female, but that does not stop her from wanting to be a king. Cimorene may be a princess, but she knows she does not want to marry a prince and become a queen. These two strong characters join forces, have many adventures and achieve their goals.

Introduction

The lack of organization in the libraries of the magical main characters factors into the plotline of Patricia C. Wrede's humorous book, *Dealing with Dragons*. Kazul, a very well-read dragon, has a large but untidy library. One of the reasons Kazul is willing to allow the strong willed Cimorene to become her captive is that the princess volunteers to organize the dragon's scroll collection. Another character, Moran, a witch, has a difficult time finding a valuable piece of information in her library because, "…the nonfiction isn't organized as well as it should be yet." If Kazul and Moran had arranged their libraries using the Dewey Decimal System they would not have had these problems!

Time Required 30–40 minutes

Objectives

- The students will review the Dewey Decimal System.

- The students will complete the activity sheet.

- The students will be able to defend the choice of "call numbers" assigned to imaginary book titles.

Materials

- visual from page 24
- activity from page 25
- pencils

Procedure

1. Introduce the lesson by asking if any student has ever read the book, *A Journey Through the Caves of Fire and Night* by DeMontmorency. Explain it is not possible to have read this book because it is a made-up title found in the book *Dealing with Dragons* by Patricia C. Wrede.

2. Explain that this lesson will involve a review of the Dewey Decimal System and the classification of ten books found in the caves of a dragon in the imaginary Kingdom of Linderwall, home of Princess Cimorene.

3. Display the visual from page 24 and review it with the students.

4. Pass out the activity from page 25. Read over the directions with the class. Allow the students to work individually or in groups.

5. Check completed worksheets with the class. It is possible that students will classify the books under different call numbers. That is expected. This lesson is an example of the process being more important than the product. The students will become more familiar with the Dewey Decimal System as they are defending their choice of call number.

Note: There may be some very literal students who insist that most of the titles belong in the 700s because they deal with magic. Allow them to do this.

Evaluation

Possible choices for call numbers:

1. Dragon and Wizard Mythology: 200s (theology, religion)

2. Archway Poets, Charms and Riddles: 800s (short stories or poems)

3. The Wizard Book Encyclopedia: 000s (encyclopedia)

4. Historia Dracorum (Dragon History): 900 (history)

5. Toads and Unicorns: 500s (living things—plants and animals)

6. Fencing Skills for Beginners: 700s (sports)

7. A Journey Through the Caves of Fire and Night: 300s (holidays)

8. Latin, the Magic Language: 400s (study of words and language)

9. Using Reverse Psychology: How to Convince a Prince: 100s (psychology)

10. Farming Fungi for Fantastic Spells: 600s (Agriculture)

Extension

Encourage the students to be creative and make up their own book titles and authors of volumes that could appear on the library shelves in a dragon's cave. The titles of the books and scrolls should reflect the content. The authors of these books should also provide a clue. For example: *Fire Prevention: Avoiding Belches, Burps and Hiccups,* by Dr. Agon could be a health book. This book would be grouped in the 600s.

Dewey Decimal System Classification

An American named Melvin Dewey devised the Dewey Decimal System in the late 1800s. This numerical system organizes the nonfiction books in the library into 10 categories of knowledge. Each book has a specific set of numbers assigned to it.

000–099 **Computer Science, Information & General Works**
[Encyclopedias, Reference Books]

100–199 **Philosophy & Psychology** *[Ethics]*

200–299 **Religion** *[Church History, Mythology, All Religions]*

300–399 **Social Sciences** *[Manners, Law, Folklore]*

400–499 **Language** *[Dictionaries, Foreign Languages]*

500–599 **Science** *[Mathematics, Chemistry, Biology]*

600–699 **Technology** *[Inventions, Health]*

700–799 **Arts & Recreation** *[Music, Sports, Hobbies, Magic]*

800–899 **Literature** *[Poetry, Plays, Short Stories]*

900–999 **History & Geography** *[Biography, Travel]*

The Library In Kazul's Cave

In *Dealing with Dragons* by Patricia C. Wrede, Kazul may be an intelligent dragon, but her library is dreadfully disorganized. Princess Cimorene has agreed to help categorize the books and scrolls found in the dragon's cave. Being well educated, Princess Cimorene knows that the Dewey Decimal System would be an excellent method to use.

Directions: The titles listed below are for imaginary books and scrolls that could be found in Kazul's collection. What call number would you assign to each book? Be prepared to defend your choice.

000–099	Computer Science, Information & General Works	500–599	Pure Science
100–199	Philosophy & Psychology	600–699	Technology
200–299	Religion	700–799	Arts & Recreation
300–399	Social Sciences	800–899	Literature
400–499	Language	900–999	History & Geography

1. Dragon and Wizard Mythology _____

2. Archway Poems, Charms and Riddles _____

3. The Wizard Book Encyclopedia _____

4. Historia Dracorum (Dragon History) _____

5. Toads and Unicorns _____

6. Fencing Skills for Beginners _____

7. A Journey Through the Caves of Fire and Night _____

8. Latin, the Magic Language _____

9. Using Reverse Psychology: How to Convince a Prince _____

10. Farming Fungi for Fantastic Spells _____

Wickedly Whimsical Words

A Dreadful Dictionary

"Perished," Mr. Poe said, "means 'killed.'"
"We know what the word 'perished' means," Klaus said, crossly. He did
know what the word "perished" meant, but he was still having trouble
understanding exactly what it was that Mr. Poe had said.
The Bad Beginning: Book the First (A Series of Unfortunate Events)

The Bad Beginning: Book the First (A Series of Unfortunate Events)

by Lemony Snicket

Story Synopsis

The "poor" Baudelaire orphans seem to go from tragedy to tragedy. First there is the terrible fire in which they lose their parents, and then comes the dreadful situation with their evil guardian, Count Olaf. Circumstances never seem to improve for 14-year-old Violet, 12-year-old Klaus and the infant, Sunny.

Introduction

Lemony Snicket, the author of A Series of Unfortunate Events books, employs a rich vocabulary in his writing. Apparently the author feels that word meaning is as important to child development as to story description. When challenging words are used, the narration stops and the words are defined. (Not all authors are so obliging.) If Mr. Snicket does not know the meaning of a word he can look it up in one of the many dictionaries found in a library. For example, he could use biographical dictionaries, foreign language dictionaries, science dictionaries and geographical dictionaries.

In this lesson the students will review dictionaries and the information included in them. Then they will be given an opportunity to create a "Wickedly Whimsical" dictionary of their own.

Time Required 40–45 minutes

Some students may choose to complete their dictionaries at home.

Objectives

- The students will review the format of dictionary entry words.

- The students will be introduced to various types of dictionaries.

- The students will learn the uses of a dictionary.
- The students will create a dictionary using invented words.

Materials

- samples of various kinds of dictionaries
- book making materials: pencils, paper, markers, construction paper, staples, scissors, etc.
- visual from page 28
- activity from page 29

Procedure

1. Prior to the lesson pull examples of various dictionaries from the library collection to share with the students during the lesson.

2. Introduce the lesson by defining a dictionary as a book of alphabetically arranged words of a language. Inform the students that they will create their own dictionary during this lesson.

3. Explain to the students that there are various kinds of dictionaries and allow them to investigate the copies you have made available.

4. Ask the students:

   What do you use a dictionary for? (Spelling and word meaning will be the most common answers.)

   What other information can you find in a dictionary? (Parts of speech, pronunciation, word history, etc.)

5. Display the visual from page 28. Review the information with the class.

6. Give each student (or group) a copy of the activity from page 29. Read the directions with the class.

7. Show the students the materials you have collected for them to use in constructing their dictionary. Encourage them to be as creative as they wish. Allow them to interact with each other as they generate definitions for the invented words listed on the activity sheet.

Evaluation

The students receive credit for their completed dictionaries. These dictionaries could be displayed on a bulletin board or table for others to enjoy.

Extension

There are many kinds of dictionaries. The students could create a detailed dictionary of their own that would be of interest to them. Their topics could include slang words, words unique to a specific movie or book series or a biographical dictionary listing the students in the class.

Wickedly Whimsical Words
A Dreadful Dictionary

In A Series of Unfortunate Events books by Lemony Snicket, Violet, Klaus and Sunny Baudelaire find that they are experiencing one miserable situation after another. Because it is difficult to find words to describe their circumstances, they create their own words and decide to write a unique dictionary. In the dictionary one can find such things as correct spelling, definitions, pronunciation, word history (etymology), parts of speech and illustrations. The word below, which can only be found in the *Dreadful Dictionary*, is an example of how words are listed in their dictionary.

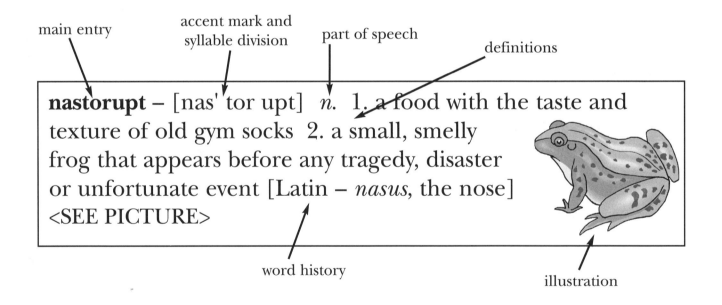

main entry

accent mark and syllable division

part of speech

definitions

nastorupt – [nas' tor upt] *n.* 1. a food with the taste and texture of old gym socks 2. a small, smelly frog that appears before any tragedy, disaster or unfortunate event [Latin – *nasus*, the nose] <SEE PICTURE>

word history

illustration

Wickedly Whimsical Words
A Dreadful Dictionary

Directions: The Baudelaire children are having a very bad time. Klaus has decided that words cannot describe the bad luck he and his sisters have experienced, so he has decided to create some words of his own. He has a feeling that these words will one day be included in a standard dictionary. Therefore, he wants to be prepared when the dictionary writers ask him for the correct spelling and definitions of the words that describe his sisters and his situation. You are going to help poor Klaus by making a new dictionary for him.

Your dictionary should:

1. Have the words listed in alphabetical order.

2. Include at least one definition for each word.

3. Have the words respelled phonetically.

4. Include the part of speech for each word.

5. Include at least 10 words from the list below.

6. Have an attractive and interesting cover.

Word List

Below is a list of invented words. You can define them any way you choose. (Remember others will be reading your definitions, so be nice!) You need only choose 10 from the list. Your dictionary will be more interesting if your words are different parts of speech. You may want to include verbs, adjectives and adverbs in with the easier nouns.

hydroate	autoflex	paripart	ouctific	snoochly	dermay
multify	morriful	synific	rupetset	slungbies	weque
benigate	creit	eupearer	gertey	outismikal	juper
kerio	lyr	ismit	perti	routue	segnal
zaget	tiffal	nixel	geflang	uppew	dewgale

Detailed Diaries
Defining Primary and Secondary Sources

"Actually, most Dinotopian writing is not even copied onto the scrolls. The hazy ideas, the gossip, the dull anecdotes, and the bad jokes are written out in a sandbox, where they can easily be erased."
Arthur Denison *Dinotopia: The Land Apart from Time*

Dinotopia: The Land Apart from Time
by James Gurney

Story Synopsis

Dinotopia: A Land Apart from Time, is written as if it were a sketchbook/journal drawn and notated by a nineteenth-century scientist. Arthur Denison, the "creator" of this document, and his son Will are shipwrecked on an incredible island where dinosaurs and humans live in harmony. The detailed notes and illustrations reveal an idyllic but isolated land.

Introduction

True research being done by young people is becoming a lost "art form." Gone are the days when students would do their reports by paraphrasing notes taken from an encyclopedia. Now, using a computer, a five-page research paper can be created in just as many minutes. Technology, usually considered a secondary source, has allowed easy access to information. However, it has diminished the ability of many students to recognize and evaluate primary source material.

Time Required 30–40 minutes

Objectives

- The students will understand the characteristics of primary and secondary sources.

- The students will complete an activity identifying primary and secondary sources.

Materials

- visual from page 32

- activity from page 33

- copy of *Dinotopia: The Land Apart from Time* by James Gurney, if available

Procedure

1. Introduce the students to the lesson by telling them that while many stories they read are narratives, sometimes authors of fiction use other types of writing to entertain and inform

their readers. Examples include letters of correspondence in *Dear Mr. Henshaw* by Beverly Cleary, journal entries in *Pedro's Journal: A Voyage With Christopher Columbus* and historical research in *Quidditch Through the Ages* by Kennilworthy Whisp, a.k.a. J. K. Rowling. (Display these books for student inspection, if available.) Explain that *Dinotopia: The Land Apart from Time* by James Gurney is an example of a fiction book written to resemble a scientific journal. This book, wonderfully illustrated by the author, contains many examples of primary source material.

2. Define primary sources as firsthand accounts communicated by someone concerning his or her experiences or observations. These methods of communication may include letters, diary entries, speeches, interviews, eyewitness news stories, photographs, legal records and artistic works concerning an event.

3. Define secondary sources as materials written after the fact. People who did not actually witness an event do this writing. These writers often gather information from a number of different primary sources. After their research, they provide analysis, explanations and reflections. Examples of secondary source materials include encyclopedias, magazines, newspaper articles and nonfiction books.

4. Display the visual. Read and discuss the types of materials listed with the students. Explain how they qualify as a primary or secondary source.

5. Give each student a copy of the activity. Read the directions to the students.

6. Inform the students that the documents listed on the worksheet could exist only in the imaginary world of Dinotopia.

Evaluation

Check the activity as a group for understanding. Be prepared for some discussion. Because the actual documents, texts and articles do not exist, it is necessary to be flexible in how the students interpret the sources.

SUGGESTED ANSWERS:

1. P	9. S
2. P	10. S
3. P	11. P
4. S	12. P
5. P	13. S
6. P	14. P
7. P	15. P
8. P	

Extension

Discuss with the students that not all sources have equal merit. Explain that the following questions should be asked when evaluating a primary or secondary source:

1. Is the source reliable?

2. Is the information up-to-date?

3. Does the date on the material matter for the type of research being done?

4. Does the author have biases? If so, what are they?

Defining Primary and Secondary Resources

Primary Sources

Firsthand accounts communicated by someone concerning his or her experiences or observations.

Primary Source Examples

- Birth Certificates
- Constitution of the United States
- Diaries
- Eyewitness Accounts
- Government Documents
- Interviews
- Last Will and Testament
- Legal Contracts
- Letters
- Photographs
- Time Capsules

Secondary Sources

Materials written after the fact.

Secondary Source Examples

- Editorials
- Encyclopedias—Print and Electronic
- Historical Novels
- Movies—e.g., *Apollo 13*
- Newspaper Articles
- Television Documentaries
- Textbooks
- U.S. History Books
- Web Site Information
- Weekly News Magazines

Detailed Diaries
Primary and Secondary Resources

Directions: The examples listed below are fictional. They are based on the imaginary world of Dinotopia, created by James Gurney. Write **P** if you think the source listed would be considered a **primary source**. Write **S** if the source would be considered a **secondary source**. Be prepared to defend your answers.

_____ 1. Arthur Denison's birth certificate.

_____ 2. The original legal charter of the Habitat Partners.

_____ 3. A poster in Cornucopia listing the winners of the Dinosaur Olympics.

_____ 4 How to Make Gold—instruction book.

_____ 5. Will Denison's diary.

_____ 6. A drawing by Arthur Denison of the unique plants found on Dinotopia.

_____ 7. Dolphin Wall Fresco (painting) located in Canyon City.

_____ 8. An ancient chart showing the caves in the World Beneath—found in the Map Room of Tentpole in the Sky.

_____ 9. A History of Dinotopia, a scroll in the library at Waterfall City.

_____ 10. A reference book: _The Care and Teaching of Humans._

_____ 11. Interview with Oolu, Skybax Instructor, concerning the care of pterosaurs.

_____ 12. Birth records of dinosaurs born at the Hatchery.

_____ 13. A feature story in the Volcaneum Gazette about a shipwreck.

_____ 14. A letter to Ambassador Bix written by Will Denison.

_____ 15. The Code of Dinotopia—engraved in stone on a pyramid wall.

A Beastly Bibliography
Citing Your Sources

"Harry Potter," said Harry.
"Are you really?" said Hermione. "I know all about you, of course—I got a few extra books for background reading, and you're in Modern Magical History, *and* The Rise and Fall of the Dark Arts *and* Great Wizarding Events of the Twentieth Century.*"*
Harry Potter and Hermione Granger *Harry Potter and the Sorcerer's Stone*

Harry Potter and the Sorcerer's Stone
by J. K. Rowling

Story Synopsis

Harry Potter and the Sorcerer's Stone is the first book in a series that chronicles the adventures of a young magician and his friends as they experience their first year at Hogwarts School for Witchcraft and Wizardry. As well as going to classes and making friends, Harry discovers the secret of the Sorcerer's Stone, fights the evil Lord Voldemort and becomes the seeker for the Gryffindor Quidditch team.

Introduction

Professor Binns is the History of Magic teacher at Hogwarts School for Witchcraft and Wizardry. He may be a very dull teacher—he is a ghost after all—but he is very meticulous. He has assigned the Gryffindor students a research paper due at the end of the term. He requires that his students thoroughly research their topics and insists that no plagiarism takes place. Therefore, each student is required to attach a bibliography at the end of the report.

Hermione Granger, Harry Potter's bookish friend, has chosen the topic, "The Influence of Magical Beasts on the History of Hogwarts." She has found the books she needs and they have some useful information in them. She knows Professor Binns will require the students to give credit to the materials used in their reports. This will be her first bibliography and she needs help.

Time Required 35–45 minutes

Objectives

- The students will discuss the importance of cited materials used in a research paper.

- The students will be introduced to a basic citation model.

- The students will create a bibliography using the information supplied.

Materials

- visuals from pages 36 and 37

- paper and pencils

- activity from page 38

- transparency marker or highlighter

Procedure

1. Introduce the lesson by reading the introduction from page 34 to the students.

2. Ask the students:

   What is a bibliography? (It is a listing, in alphabetical order, of materials used in a report. It is also known as a "works cited" page.)

   What is plagiarism? (Plagiarism is copying the work of another person and using it as if it was your own.)

3. Inform the students that they are going to learn to create a bibliography. Explain that when they do a report, it is important that they are capable of correctly giving credit to the people whose ideas they use.

4. Display the visual from page 36. Explain that there is a format for the information. The format used in this lesson will be:

   Author (last name, first name). Title. Place Published: Publisher, Copyright Date.

5. Keep the visual displayed throughout the lesson so the students can use it for reference.

6. Pass out the activity, lined paper and pencils.

7. Read the directions to the students at the top of the activity.

8. Allow 10–15 minutes to complete the activity.

9. Display, discuss and correct work using the visual from page 37. Students are encouraged to correct any errors they made. (Were they able to decode the Roman numeral CMXLV?)

Evaluation

Students are given credit for participation in the lesson. This lesson is often taught in collaboration with the classroom teacher as a precursor to a research paper.

Extension

Often students writing a report or a research paper will have discovered interesting material in several books written by the same author. The visual on page 39 addresses this situation. Display the visual and ask the students the question at the top of the page. After some discussion, the students should be able to reason that the titles of the books need to be put in alphabetical order. The title pages in this visual may also be added to the three on the activity sheet if the lesson needs to be extended.

Note: *The objective of the lesson is to introduce the student to the fundamentals of citing books written by one author with the hope that the student will be able to apply the skill in a practical way. The advanced student may be curious about how to cite reference books, Web sites and periodicals. Be prepared and have a good writing handbook available to refer to if these questions should arise.*

Bibliography
Sample Entry

author, last name first

comma

period

Underline the title.

period

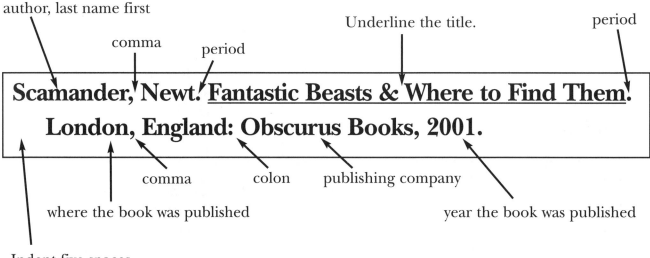

Scamander, Newt. <u>Fantastic Beasts & Where to Find Them</u>.

London, England: Obscurus Books, 2001.

comma

colon

publishing company

where the book was published

year the book was published

Indent five spaces
for the second line.

Bibliography
The Influence of Magical Beasts on the History of Hogwarts

Bagshot, Bathilda. <u>A History of Hogwarts</u>.
Hogsmeade, Scotland: Medieval Press, 1884.

Jigger, Arsenives. <u>Magical Beasts of Long Ago</u>.
London, England: Alchemy Publications, 1945.

Waffling, Adelbert. <u>Exploring Monsters in
History</u>. Salem, Massachusetts: Witchworks
Press, 1771.

A Beastly Bibliography
Giving Credit Where Credit Is Due

Directions: Below are copies of the title pages in the books Hermione used to do her report. Using your own paper, create the bibliography for this report.

A History
of Hogwarts
by
Bathilda Bagshot

Medieval Press
Hogsmeade, Scotland
1884

Magical Beasts
of Long Ago

by
Arsenives Jigger

CMXLV
Alchemy Publications
1443 Nocturnal Alley
London, England

Exploring Monsters
in History

by
Adelbert Waffling

Printed in 1771
Witchworks Press
Salem, Massachusetts

What to Do?

The same author wrote these books. How would you cite them in your bibliography?

Holidays with Hags
by
Gilderoy Lockhart

1978
Ego Publishing
Diagon Alley
London, England

Travels with Trolls
by
Gilderoy Lockhart

1981
Ego Publishing
Diagon Alley
London, England

Talking to a Troll
The Interview Process

"Yes, yes my dear sir—and I do know your name, Mr. Bilbo Baggins. And you do know my name, though you don't remember that I belong to it. I am Gandalf, and Gandalf means me! To think that I should have lived to be good-morninged by Belladonna Took's son, as if I was selling buttons at the door!"
Gandalf the Grey *The Hobbit, or, There and Back Again*

The Hobbit, or, There and Back Again
by J. R. R. Tolkien

Story Synopsis

Bilbo Baggins is your typical Hobbit. He is short and stocky and has wonderfully hairy feet. When an old friend of his father, Gandalf the Grey, appears, he has no idea of the adventures he is about to undertake. On his journey he meets trolls, elves, men and orcs. He outsmarts a dragon and finds a lost ring. When he returns home over a year later, he is a changed Hobbit. He has no idea that the ring he now has in his possession played an important part in the destruction of the Third Age of Middle-earth. He also has no way of knowing what the consequences of ownership of the ring will mean to his nephew, Frodo.

Introduction

An interview is a series of questions and answers between two or more people. The purpose of an interview is an exchange of information concerning a specific issue. In this lesson the students will read and discuss a sample interview in which a troll is interviewed concerning an incident that turned his friends into stone. (The interview is based on events that take place in Chapter 2, "Roast Mutton," of J. R. R. Tolkien's *The Hobbit*.) The students will then create a whimsical interview of their own in which they will ask an imaginary creature questions concerning the creature's habits and/or hobbies.

Time Required 35–45 minutes

Objectives

- The students will be able to define an interview and describe its characteristics.

- The students will participate in the interview process.

Materials

- pencils

- visual from page 42

- activity from page 43 (one per group)

Procedure

1. Introduce the lesson by displaying the sample interview from the visual and reading it with the class.

2. Explain to the students that even though the interview between the interviewer from *Monster Monthly Magazine* and Tom the Troll was cut short, we still learned a great deal from the conversation that did take place.

3. Ask the students: What do we learn about the length of an interview? (It can be any length.) When does the interviewer think of the questions to ask? (In advance.) Can the interview take an unexpected turn? (Yes, this one had to be continued later due to the approaching dawn.) Does an interview always take place in person? (No, modern technology can be used.) What are some of the reasons interviews are conducted? (Curiosity about the interviewee, eyewitness information, job interview, etc.)

4. Group the students into teams of two to three students.

5. Give each team an activity sheet and explain the directions. Stress that the questions should concern the habits and/or hobbies of the creature. An example might be:

   INTERVIEWER: Mr. Dragon, your habit of throwing flames from your nostrils can be very destructive. Do you ever try to control this habit when you are around others?

   DRAGON: This habit can be a nuisance. It really "burns up" some of my friends.

6. Ask the students if there are any questions and allow them 15 minutes to complete the activity.

7. Call on volunteers to present their interviews. (Some will be VERY funny.) The presentations take between one to three minutes apiece.

8. Conclude the lesson with a class discussion concerning the importance of the interview process in today's society. To stimulate discussion, ask questions such as:

If you could interview one person, who would it be and why?

Other than journalism, can you think of any other professions that would use an interview? (Possible answers: law enforcement, employment agencies, news media and marketing firms.)

Evaluation

Critique each presentation using the criteria on the worksheet. The scoring is subjective. Most groups earn between 95% and 100%.

Extension

The bias of an interviewer is often evident in the questions that are asked of the subject. For example, if the principal asked a student if this was the first time she had thrown a paper airplane in class, it would seem that the fact that the student did throw the airplane was precluded.

Have the students write two sets of questions for the same person to be interviewed. (This person may be real or imaginary.) One set of questions would show that the interviewer was a supporter of the person being interviewed. The second set of questions would demonstrate a dislike for the interviewee.

For example, if a student were to interview Bilbo Baggins concerning his adventures in the Misty Mountains, they might ask the question two different ways:

- INTERVIEWER (Friend): Bilbo, what is it like having so many grand adventures with your wonderful friend the wizard, Gandalf the Grey?

- INTERVIEWER (Foe): Bilbo, why do you think Gandalf tricked you into becoming a burglar and traveling all that distance with 13 selfish and ungrateful dwarfs?

The Interview

An interview is a series of questions and answers between two or more people. The purpose of an interview is to exchange information concerning a specific issue.

Sample Interview

Interviewer: Good evening, Ted. I appreciate the opportunity you have given me to conduct this interview. As you know, I am a reporter for *Monster Monthly Magazine.* This meeting was set up to take place after a big meal so that you would not view me as a possible entrée. You know I will be asking questions to try to discover what really happened to your friends, the trolls Tom, Bert and Bill.

Ted the Troll: (burping) Tom, Bert and Bill turned into stone.

Interviewer: Yes, we know. But how did it happen?

TT: (grunting) Me not sure. But me real mad.

Interviewer: So you are upset that your friends are no longer with us?

TT: They are here, just stone. Me mad because some sneak broke into cave and took all good gold and shiny things.

Interviewer: Very interesting. Do you know what else was in that cave?

TT: Me cannot talk now. Sun be up soon. Me do not want to be stone like the others. Us can talk when sun goes back down.

Interviewer: That will be fine. We can meet here tomorrow night or we can continue this conversation from your cave using your cell phone. I still want to find out if you think there was any foul play in what happened to your friends.

TT: Foul play? Good idea! Bring fowl next time. Ted likes chicken.

Talking to Trolls

Directions: Working in groups, create at least five questions to ask one of the imaginary creatures listed below. Then make up the answers you think your interviewee would give! The purpose of the interview is to find information for an article you are writing for *Monster Monthly Magazine,* titled "Interesting Habits and Hobbies." Be prepared to share your interview with the class.

* **Centaur**—an intelligent beast who is half-man and half-horse.

* **Dragon**—a monstrous winged and scaly reptile.

* **Elf**—a small, mischievous being having human form and magic powers.

* **Giant**—a being of great stature and strength.

* **Hobbit**—a short and stout fun-loving being with hairy feet.

* **Troll**—a supernatural creature dwelling in caves or hills.

* **Your Choice**

Your interview will be scored using the following criteria:	
1. Interesting questions that deal with the topic.	up to 25 points
2. Appropriate answers to the questions.	up to 25 points
3. Group participation.	up to 25 points
4. Presentation of interview.	up to 25 points

Redwall's Riddles
Choosing the Best Reference Tool

Old Brother Methuselah had kept the Abbey records for as long as any creature could remember. It was his life's work and consuming passion. Beside the official chronicle of Redwall, he also kept his own personal volume, full of valuable information.
Redwall

Redwall
by Brian Jacques

Story Synopsis

The kindhearted and peaceful mice inhabiting Redwall Abbey realize that their lives in Mossflower Wood are about to change dramatically. The army of the evil one-eyed rat, Cluny the Scourge, is planning to invade their home. The mice believe that the powerful sword of the legendary hero Martin the Warrior is the only thing that can save them. Unfortunately the sword has been hidden away and not even the ancient scholar Methuselah has knowledge of its whereabouts. It is the young apprentice Matthias who gathers up his courage and sets off on the perilous quest to find the hidden sword.

Introduction

There are many riddles that need to be solved if Redwall Abbey is going to be saved from the invading horde of scavenger rats. The wise old mouse Methuselah knows a well-educated person does not necessarily know the answer to every riddle, but knows where to find the information

needed to solve them. This lesson will encourage students to be more aware of the resources available to them as they continue on their educational journey.

Time Required 30–40 minutes

Objectives

- The students will review various reference tools.

- The students will use knowledge of these reference materials.

- The students will employ strategic critical thinking skills while participating in a teacher-directed review activity.

Materials

- examples of the following: almanac, atlas, biography, cookbook, dictionary, encyclopedia, globe, grammar book, magazines, newspapers, telephone directory, thesaurus, time-table, world record book

- visual from page 47

- bingo game card from page 48

- bingo cards from pages 49 and 50

- bingo markers

Procedure

1. Prior to the lesson:

    - Collect examples of the listed reference books to use in the beginning of the lesson.

    - Photocopy the appropriate number of bingo game cards.

    - Photocopy the game cards and cut them out.

2. Explain to the students that a quick review will be necessary to prepare them for the activity.

3. Display the visual. Show an example of each item as you review the list.

4. Ask the students if they know how to play bingo. Explain that today's activity will be similar to that game, requiring them to fill in the boxes of a grid in a horizontal, vertical or diagonal row.

5. Pass out a game card and markers to each student.

6. Tell them to look over the grid. Explain that, unlike bingo where each card is different, they all have the same information on their cards. This is because there are several possible answers for each of the cards.

7. Explain that you will read a question. They should put a marker over a resource that would have the information in question. There are often several places that the information could be found, but only <u>one</u> box may be marked at a time. (Students should be prepared to defend their choice if it is different from the ones listed on the selected card.)

8. Cite the following example: "Suppose I chose the card 'Where would you find information about Brian Jacques, the author of the Redwall series?'" Then solicit answers. (Students might answer: an encyclopedia, a biography, magazine article, etc.) Accept all logical answers, but remind the students that they may only mark <u>one</u> box at a time.

9. Point out that "encyclopedia" is listed multiple times. Ask the students why they think that is. (An encyclopedia contains general knowledge.)

10. Begin the game by requiring the students to write the title of their favorite book in the free space. (The main reason for this is to satisfy your curiosity about what the students are reading. It also sets the tone for the game.)

11. Continue by telling the class that when a student has marked five boxes in a row, he may call out "magic." This is because finding the information one is looking for is indeed magic.

12. Shuffle the cards and randomly choose one. Read the statement on the card to the students. You may want to read each card twice.

13. Ask for volunteers to tell you what tool they selected. You may also read the references suggested on the card and inquire if anyone had a different choice. (If so, ask them to explain. The students are often aware of articles appearing in current periodicals.)

14 Continue this process until a student calls "magic." This may occur after just five or six cards have been read. The game can be continued after the first winners are identified.

Evaluation

If time allows, an informal "debriefing" may take place after the activity. Ask the students the following questions to stimulate a discussion:

1. What did you like about the game?

2. What did you dislike about the game?

3. Did you think it was fair? Why or why not?

4. Do you think that almost all of the answers to the cards could have been found on the Internet? Why or why not?

5. What do you think the most valuable research tool is?

Extension

Making learning fun makes learning easier. Encourage the students to create games of their own using a theme that might otherwise be "dry" and "boring." These games can be card games, board games, class competitions or fun puzzles. You never know, they may use their artistic talent or computer skills to create the next national pastime!

Research Tools

* **Almanac:** an annual publication containing statistics, data and general information.

* **Atlas:** a book of maps.

* **Biography:** the story of a person's life.

* **Cookbook:** a book of recipes and instructions concerning food preparation.

* **Dictionary:** a book containing words and their meanings.

* **Encyclopedias:** books, organized alphabetically, containing information on many subjects.

* **Internet:** information accessed using a computer and the World Wide Web.

* **Globe:** a model of the earth.

* **Grammar Book:** a text containing rules of a written language.

* **Magazines:** a periodical publication focused on a specific topic or interest.

* **Newspapers:** current events publications.

* **Telephone Directory:** a listing of local telephone numbers and addresses.

* **Thesaurus:** a book of words, a lexicon.

* **Timetable:** a graphic displaying history chronologically.

* **World Record Book:** a periodical observing unique achievements.

Magic Bingo

Directions: Place a marker in the box that contains a resource that could be used to locate the information in the "Where would you find…" statement. There are often several reference tools that might have the information, but only <u>one</u> box may be marked at a time. *(Be prepared to defend your choice if it is different from the ones listed on the selected card.)*

M	A	G	I	C
atlas	biography	*Guinness Book of World Records*	globe	local newspaper
thesaurus	encyclopedia	almanac	dictionary	encyclopedia
encyclopedia	*Sports Illustrated* magazine	**Free Space** *(Fill in title of your favorite book.)* _____	grammar handbook	Internet Web site
dictionary	eyewitness interview	encyclopedia	*Newsweek* magazine	*The Timetables of History* reference book
People magazine	cookbook	telephone directory	encyclopedia	card catalog (patron's catalog)

Magic Bingo
"Where would you find..." Cards

... a map of Peru? (atlas, encyclopedia, globe, almanac)	**... information about Thomas Jefferson?** (biography, Internet, encyclopedia, almanac)	**... details about the tallest person in the world?** (*Guinness Book of World Records*, encyclopedia)
... what countries bordered the Black Sea? (atlas, encyclopedia, globe, almanac)	**... what the score was for yesterday's Little League baseball game?** (local newspaper, interview)	**... words to make a poem you wrote more descriptive?** (thesaurus, dictionary)
... pictures of flags for a report you are doing on South America? (almanac, encyclopedia, Internet)	**... what the word "quixotic" means?** (dictionary, thesaurus, encyclopedia)	**... when the first automobile was invented?** (encyclopedia, *Timetables of History*)
... what the first words were that Neil Armstrong spoke on the moon? (encyclopedia, Internet, biography)	**... what teams will play in the next Super Bowl?** (*Sports Illustrated*, newspaper, Internet)	**... the definition of a paragraph?** (grammar handbook, dictionary)

… what television programs had the highest rating last week? (Internet, newspaper, *Newsweek*)	… how to pronounce "phlegm"? (dictionary, encyclopedia)	… who was at fault for the car accident that happened in front of the school? (eyewitness, local newspaper)
… who painted the *Mona Lisa*? (encyclopedia, Internet)	… if the president was out of the country last week? (*Newsweek*, Internet)	… when Lewis and Clark arrived at the Pacific Ocean? (*Timetables of History*, encyclopedia)
… who the most popular rock star in the United States is? (*People* magazine, Internet)	… how to make tuna casserole? (cookbook, Internet)	… where you can get pizza tonight? (telephone book, newspaper)
… who wrote *James and the Giant Peach*? (card catalog, encyclopedia, Internet)	… on what date New Year's Day will fall next year? (almanac, encyclopedia)	… when Cleopatra lived? (encyclopedia, *Timetables of History*, biography)
… the direction that Ohio is in from your current location? (atlas, encyclopedia, globe, almanac)	… the difference between a verb and an adverb? (grammar book, dictionary)	… where to contact a good dentist? (telephone directory, Internet, interview)

Research to the Rescue
Investigating Indexes

Thornmallow looked around. The library had walls of books. There were books on the windowsills and books stacked two- and three- and four deep on the shelves. Where there were no books, single pieces of parchment littered the floor, covered with crabbed writings and odd diagrams with arrows pointing up and down and around great circles.
Wizard's Hall

Wizard's Hall
by Jane Yolen

Story Synopsis

Young Henry is renamed Thornmallow when he shows up at Wizard's Hall, a training school for young wizards. He is the 113th student to be admitted. This fact plays a significant part in the story. He and his new friends, Will, Gorse and Tansy, have a big task in front of them. They must defeat the wicked wizard Nettle and his nasty beast, the patchwork dragon, to rescue the teachers and students of Wizard's Hall. With information that they researched in Wizard's Hall's library, they manage to defeat the evildoers. All ends well when Thornmallow realizes he is an "enhancer" rather than an "enchanter" and that this is a very good thing to be.

Introduction

When Henry arrives at Wizard's Hall he is renamed Thornmallow. (His new name means prickly on the outside and squishy within.) He no sooner gets acclimated to his surroundings than it is revealed that a disgruntled former teacher and his smelly beast will soon attack the school. On a quest to find out how to defeat this menace, our hero is taken by his friends to a place they hope will hold the answer to their questions. They know that knowledge is power and the best place to obtain this knowledge is from a library book!

Time Required 35–40 minutes

Objectives

- The students will define an index.

- The students will understand the purposes of an index.

- The students will complete an activity sheet related to the information found in an index.

Materials

- visual from page 54
- activity from page 55
- pencils

Procedure

1. Display the visual. Read the first two paragraphs to the class.

2. Direct the students to the sample index and ask them the following questions:

   How are the entry words listed? *(alphabetically)*

   On what pages would information about capturing creatures be found? *(53–65)*

   Would it be possible to find out how to get to the enchanted forest? *(Yes, there is a map on page 68.)*

   If more information about defeating spells was needed, it would be necessary to look under the "M" in this index. Why? *(The researcher is directed to see "magical sayings." This is called cross-referencing.)*

   Would it be possible to find illustrations of beasts in this book? *(Yes, on pages 45–48.)*

3. Ask the students if they have any questions.

4. Distribute the activity. Read the directions to the students. They may work individually or in groups.

Evaluation

The answers to the activity sheet should be checked and discussed as a group.

On what page(s) would you find...

1. A description of a quilt? *(25)*

2. Information about the history of Wizard's Hall? *(52–73)*

3. A photograph of Magister Hickory? *(122)*

4. Facts about the faculty at Wizard's Hall? *(65–68)*

5. What a white nettle is? *(189)*

6. In what order are items listed in an index? *(alphabetically)*

7. In what kind of books are indexes found? *(Possible answers: nonfiction, text books, reference books, informational books.)*

8. What purposes do indexes serve? *(Possible answers: to find if specific information is located in the book, locate page numbers, identify illustrations.)*

9. What listing is usually more helpful if specific information is needed, an index or a table of contents? *(index)* Why? *(Possible answer: It is more specific to content and amount of information on a specific topic.)*

10. Other than page numbers, what kind of information is given in an index? *(Possible answers: the location of photographs, illustrations and maps, correct spelling, cross-references.)*

Extension

Students like to be risk takers. Let them enjoy taking a chance. Display a list of unrelated topics. Allow the students to pick a topic, go directly to the shelves, choose a book that they think has that topic in it and return to their seat with the unopened book. There they may open the book and see if it contains an index that lists information about the topic. They only get one chance. (They get three points if their selection contains an index, two points if it lists the topic in the index and one point if there is an illustration or photograph of the topic in the body of the book.)

This is a FUN activity. However, be forewarned! The library will be chaotic for a short time. The books not checked out will need to be put back on the shelves. On the plus side, the students will become more familiar with the nonfiction section of the library. Besides, they may select books that have not been off the shelves in years.

Sample Topics

American flag	Mayflower
Argentina	Nile River
bagpipes	oak trees
coffee	raccoon
gold	radio
Gulf of Mexico	telephone
Hank Aaron	Thomas Jefferson
icebergs	transcontinental railroad
Incas	trumpets
Johnny Appleseed	Tyrannosaurus Rex
Mars	United Nations
volcanoes	weather satellites

Research to the Rescue
Investigating Indexes

In Jane Yolen's book, *Wizard's Hall*, Thornmallow and his friends do their best to help defend Wizard's Hall from the wicked wizard, Nettle. They visit the library looking for books that contain information about defeating magical beasts. The students have very little time and need to use it as wisely as possible. What should they do?

They could look in a book's index to see if it has the information they are looking for. An index, found in the back of informational books, is an alphabetical listing of all the important subjects found in it. The index lists topics and page numbers. Sometimes topics are cross-referenced and information concerning illustrations is included.

Sample index from the imaginary book *Defeating Magical Creatures*:

beasts, 1–23
    domesticated, 14–18
    history of, 11–13
    types, *[illus.]*, 45–48
capturing creatures, 53–65
    containment, 55
    magical methods, 57–58
    traps, 60–64

defeating spells, 122–199
    also see: magical sayings
    chants, 132–142
    rhymes, 190–199
enchanted forest, 67–95
    inhabitants, 67–72
    location, *[map]*, 68
    warnings concerning, 70–72

Research to the Rescue
Investigating Indexes

Directions: The box below contains part of an index from a book Thornmallow thinks might help him in his research. Use it to answer the questions.

correspondence, *see connections*	red, 189–192
Hickory, Magister, 122–134	white, 189
Castle of the Devine, 133	**quilts,** 25–29
early years, *[photo]*, 122	care of, 29
education, 125	description of, 25
family, 127	sample patterns, *[illus.]*, 26–28
founding of Wizard's Hall, 130	unstitching, 28
spell-making, 233	**Wizard's Hall,** 52–73
nettles, 189–200	design, *[interior map]*, 56
blind, 190, 197	history, 52–58
deaf, 197	faculty, 65–68
false, 199	student body, 72—73

On what page(s) would you find...

1. A description of a quilt? _____

2. Information about the history of Wizard's Hall? _____

3. A photograph of Magister Hickory? _____

4. Facts about the faculty at Wizard's Hall? _____

5. What a white nettle is? _____

Answer these questions

6. In what order are items listed in an index? _____

7. In what kind of books are indexes found? _____

8. What purposes do indexes serve? _____

9. What listing is usually more helpful if specific information is needed, an index or a table of contents? _____ Why? _____

10. Other than page numbers, what kind of information is given in an index?
    _____

"Tra-la-laaa!"
Instant Stories
Plot, Character, Setting and Theme

You'd better straighten up, young man, because you can't spend
the rest of your life making silly books.
Former teacher of Dav Pilkey, author of *The Adventures of Captain Underpants*

The Adventures of Captain Underpants
by Dav Pilkey

Story Synopsis

Who is this pudgy caped crusader whose adventures are chronicled in word and picture by the ever-adolescent Dav Pilkey? Why, it's Principal Krupp of Jerome Horwitz Elementary School, of course! Hypnotized by two fourth graders, our unaware, "underwear" hero quickly transforms into a superhero who can easily defeat the evil Dr. Diaper.

Introduction

A good story is like magic, but can you put into words why you liked it so well? Could it be the fantastic plot? Maybe it's the fascinating characters involved in an out of the ordinary time and place. The following activity will define the elements of a story and allow the students to be creative as they conjure up masterpieces of their own.

Time Required 40–45 minutes

Objectives

- The students will become familiar with the literary terms of plot, character, setting and theme.

- The students will create a unique story.

- The students will be able to discuss the elements of a story in literary terms.

Materials

- visual from page 58

- activity from page 59

- activity cards from page 60–63

- pencils

- extra lined paper

Note: *The cards work best when duplicated on card stock, a different color for each of the literary elements.*

Procedure

1. Prior to the lesson, photocopy and cut out the activity cards.

2. Introduce the lesson by displaying the visual and reading it with the class. (Note: *Cinderella* is used in the examples because of students' familiarity with it and its many versions.)

3. Group the students into creative teams of three or four students.

4. Instruct the students that they are going to be part of a team that just may create a new best-selling novel.

5. Give each group a copy of the activity.

6. Allow each team to choose a card for each of the elements. (To allow for random selection, turn them face down or enclose them in an envelope.)

7. Explain that the story they create must include the elements that were selected. Their product does not need to be a polished manuscript. However, at the end of the creative period they will be expected to share their progress with the class.

8. Allow 15–20 minutes for the creative writing process.

9. Ask the students to share their stories with the class.

10. Discuss why most of their stories were humorous. (They should conclude that it is because of the arbitrary connections of the chosen plot, characters, setting and theme.)

11. Encourage students to use the literary terms of the lesson in their speaking and writing.

Evaluation

This activity is an example of a lesson where the process is more important than the product. Therefore, the students are required to evaluate their own work. A "Literary Rating" scale can be found at the bottom of the activity sheet. The students should be informed that they receive full credit for the completion of the assignment and that the rating they attach to their work has no reflection on their grade.

Extension

Display a list of well-known traditional tales. (Examples: Beauty and the Beast, Goldilocks and the Three Bears, Little Red Riding Hood, The Ugly Duckling, Robin Hood.) Ask the students to identify the plot, setting, characters and themes for these stories. Discuss the differences and similarities of the story elements of the selected tales.

Hocus Pocus
Instant Stories

Definitions and Examples

PLOT—the action of the story

The universal plot of *Cinderella* is:
"mistreated girl overcomes hardships with the help of a magical being."

CHARACTERS—the "beings" in the story

The characters in *Cinderella* sometimes include:
a cruel stepmother, a fairy godmother and some talking mice.

SETTING—the place and time of the story

The setting of *Cinderella* often is:
in a magical kingdom long, long ago…

THEME—the subject or message of the story

The theme of *Cinderella* is:
goodness and determination will be rewarded.

Hocus Pocus
Instant Stories

Name(s)_____ Date: _____ Literary Rating: _____

Directions: Choose a plot, character, setting and theme card. Use these cards to create a story. Be prepared to share your story with the class. At the conclusion of the lesson, you are responsible for evaluating your work. Use the Literary Rating scale below and assign yourself the "stars" you think your creation has earned.

Story

_____

_____

_____

_____

_____

_____

_____

_____

_____

_____

_____

_____

_____

_____

Continue on back if necessary.

Literary Rating

**** This is the beginning of a best-selling novel.

*** This story has potential, but needs some work.

** Only one of the story elements is working well, changes are needed.

* No hope!

Hocus Pocus
Plot Cards

A person runs away from home, trying to find true happiness.	A hurricane is in the forecast and a group of school children is stranded on a broken-down school bus.
Mother has left for the day. Those remaining at home know that they will be in big trouble if they do not clean up their terrible mess.	Students are caught cheating on a major test. Should they be punished?
Who is responsible for the bank robbery and why did they do it?	Best friends are moving away from each other. How will they cope?
A magic lamp is found. Will three wishes be granted?	Something terrible goes wrong and the spacecraft cannot get back to Earth.

Hocus Pocus
Character Cards

Bobby Jo: a young rascal **Jo Bob:** a goody-goody	**Charlie:** a sad circus clown **Mr. Frank:** a rich man
Smokey: a big black dog **Sammy:** a lonely girl	**Scott:** a football player **Ray:** a newspaper editor **Mr. Kirk:** the principal
Pat: a policeman **Milo:** a magician	**Angie:** a computer whiz **Polly:** a talkative parrot **Mrs. Anderson:** Angie's mother
Lucy: a three-year-old girl **Matthew:** her baby-sitter	**Willard Williams:** an astronaut **Doris Dennis:** an artist **Connie Jones:** a teenager

Hocus Pocus
Setting Cards

Place: a haunted house **Time**: a dark winter's night	**Place**: a fast food restaurant **Time**: during lunch
Place: Hollywood, California **Time**: Valentine's Day	**Place**: a football field **Time**: one hour before the big game
Place: Old McDonald's farm **Time**: three years ago	**Place**: in between a rock and a hard place **Time**: the present
Place: a factory **Time**: in the near future	**Place**: a castle in Ireland **Time**: long ago

Hocus Pocus

Theme Cards

Make new friends, but keep the old.	It is better to be right than to be rich.
Life is like a box of chocolates, you never know what you are going to get.	If you are kind to others, they will be kind to you.
The strong and quick will always win.	Beauty is skin deep.
When bad things happen, it is better to laugh than to feel sorry for yourself.	If you are willing to take a risk, you should be willing to pay the price.

Dire Dilemmas
Foreshadowing and Flashback

I'm sure you would know, even if I didn't tell you, that things were about to get much worse for the Baudelaires, but I will end this chapter with the moment of companionable comfort rather than skip ahead to the unpleasant events of the next morning, or the terrible trials of the days that followed, or the horrific crime that marked the end of the Baudelaires' time at Prufrock Prep.
Lemony Snicket *The Austere Academy: Book the Fifth*

The Austere Academy: Book the Fifth
A Series of Unfortunate Events

by Lemony Snicket

Story Synopsis

Book Five in the A Series of Unfortunate Events saga finds the Baudelaire orphans as mistreated and miserable as ever. They have again escaped the evil Count Olaf only to find that they have been enrolled in Prufrock Preparatory School, without a doubt the worst boarding school in existence. Here they are forced to live in a bug-infected shack, attend boring classes taught by terrible teachers and suffer the constant insults of Carmelita Spats. Just when they think things cannot get any worse, Count Olaf shows up disguised as the world's finest gym teacher. The three anxious orphans can only guess what scheme he has concocted to rob them of their inheritance.

Introduction

Lemony Snicket, the author of the A Series of Unfortunate Events books, uses flashback and foreshadowing masterfully. The stories, which are rather morose in content, are written in a "tongue-in-cheek" style. The reader knows this because just when things are too sad to endure, the author flashes back to a happier time in the life of his three main characters, Violet, Klaus and Sunny Baudelaire. The author also prepares the reader for events that will soon be developing in the story by informing the reader that even though he is reluctant to convey the upcoming information, he is duty bound to do so.

Time Required 30–40 minutes

Objectives

• The students will be introduced to the literary terms of foreshadowing and flashback.

• The students will be involved in an interactive activity that will reinforce the concepts introduced.

Materials

- visual from page 66
- tic-tac-toe board from page 67
- activity cards from pages 68 and 69
- transparency marker or highlighter

Procedure

1. Prior to the lesson, photocopy the activity cards and have them cut and ready for class. (Keep a master copy of the cards for use in identifying the correct answers.)

2. Display the visual from page 66. Read the information on it to the students.

3. Ask the students if they can recall ever having read stories that used foreshadowing or flashback. (Flashback tends to be easier for the students to identify. Foreshadowing can be subtle and is not as identifiable.)

4. Divide the students into two groups.

5. Explain that they are going to play tic-tac-toe using information about foreshadowing and flashbacks. Decide which group will be the X group and which will be the O group.

6. Display the tic-tac-toe board from page 67, explain the directions and rules.

   Directions: A foreshadowing or flashback card will be drawn from the deck of cards and read to the first group. The group must correctly identify the card as foreshadowing or flashback. If they are correct, they may place their team's mark on the grid. If they are incorrect, it is the next team's turn. Continue playing until one team has three X's or O's in a row.

7. Start the game. The group with the oldest student in it goes first.

Evaluation

After the game is completed and a winning team has been established, there may be a few game cards remaining. To check for understanding, read them to the students to see if they can identify them correctly.

Extension

Encourage the students to create their own foreshadowing and flashback cards to be used in the class tic-tac-toe game. They may think of other games in which the concepts of foreshadowing and flashback can be reinforced. The library may wish to sponsor a game development contest.

The students creating the games would be allowed time in the library to demonstrate how they are played to other students.

Foreshadowing and Flashback

Foreshadowing

When a writer **foreshadows** an event he or she uses clues or hints to tip off the reader that something which has just occurred is going to matter later. **Foreshadowing** is one of the ways a writer generates anticipation for what is coming up next in the story.

> But they should have been more nervous about their plan, and about what would happen that evening when the sun set on the brown lawn and the luminous circle began to glow. They should have been nervous in their regular shoes, about what would happen when they were in each other's.

An example of foreshadowing from *The Austere Academy: Book the Fifth (A Series of Unfortunate Events)* by Lemony Snicket. *(The author is giving clues to the reader that the Baudelaire children and the Quagmire triplets are going to be in big trouble in the future.)*

Flashback

A writer uses a **flashback** when he or she wants the reader to be aware of something that happened before the story began. **Flashbacks** offer information about the characters' current situation or make clear why certain things happen in a story. When a flashback takes place, the chain of events in a story is interrupted.

> "Remember the picnic?" Violet said. "We were going to Rutabaga River for a picnic, and Father was so excited about the meal he made that he forgot to pack silverware!"
>
> "Of course I remember," Klaus said. "We had to eat all that sweet-and-sour shrimp with our hands."

An example of a flashback from *The Austere Academy: Book the Fifth (A Series of Unfortunate Events)* by Lemony Snicket. *(Violet is remembering happier times. She is using a funny event from the past to try to make her brother and sister feel better about receiving the punishment of having to eat their meals without silverware.)*

Dire Dilemma Tic-Tac-Toe

Directions:

1. Identify the card as an example of foreshadowing or flashback.

2. If you are correct, place an X or O on the grid. If you are incorrect, it is the next team's turn.

3. The pattern repeats until one group has successfully gotten three X's or O's in a row.

Dire Dilemma Tic-Tac-Toe
Foreshadowing Cards

Little did Jim know that what he had done was going to make a big difference in the game.	Afterwards, Sandy would remember the warning her mother had given her that morning.	Hunter would later wish that the clothes he packed had been for a colder climate.
Clapping her hands for joy would be the last happy thing Katie would do for a very long time.	Three tragic events had happened this week. Things will surely change now he thought.	No one entering that cave had ever returned to tell what he or she had found.
Even though the forecast was for clear weather, heavy snow started to fall.	The owl hooted three times that night. Was that a signal of events to come?	He put the book on the shelf. Later he wished he had read it from cover to cover.

Dire Dilemma Tic-Tac-Toe
Flashback Cards

He remembered a time when he was younger and happier.	What had just happened reminded Terry of an event from his childhood.	When she went to bed that night her dreams were of her seventh birthday when…
The strong smell of smoke reminded Chris of the time, long ago when…	As fast as he was running forward, his memories were racing just as fast backward.	She was tired and hungry, and her mind started to recollect happier times.
He reminisced about the good times before the war.	What had taken place in the kitchen just now had started three years ago.	That story brought to mind one he had heard when he was a child away at summer camp.

Creepy Creatures
Compare and Contrast

The creatures, some sitting in chairs, others reclining on a sofa, were watching him intently.... Every one of these "creatures" was at least as big as James himself, and in the strange greenish light that shone down from somewhere in the ceiling, they were absolutely terrifying to behold.
James and the Giant Peach

James and the Giant Peach
by Roald Dahl

Story Synopsis

James Henry Trotter, orphaned when an angry rhinoceros (recently escaped from the London Zoo) kills his beloved parents, is the hero of this whimsical tale about overcoming hardships. Upon the death of his parents James is sent to live with his cruel aunts. While hiding behind some bushes in the garden the mistreated young boy is approached by an odd-looking stranger who gives him a bag of magic crystals.

James accidentally drops the bag and the result is a fruit tree with an enormous peach growing on it. A set of circumstances leads James inside the peach to find it inhabited by some large and very verbal insects including an earthworm, a grasshopper, a spider, a centipede and a ladybug. While inside the peach, James and his new friends escape the confines of the garden. They roll to the Atlantic Ocean, and eventually make a grand arrival in New York City. There they settle into pleasant lives.

Introduction

Like most of Roald Dahl's characters, those in *James and the Giant Peach* are not the least bit understated. Our hero, James Henry Trotter, is good, brave and very smart. Our villains, Aunt Sponge and Aunt Spike, are lazy, greedy and very stupid. The contrast between nephew and aunts is evident. The aunts can be contrasted also. They are alike in personality and purpose but their physical appearance is very different—Sponge is as fat as Spike is thin.

In this lesson students will create a list of characteristics of some of the creatures in *James and the Giant Peach*. They will then place the items from their list on a diagram that will allow them to see the differences and similarities of their chosen creatures. Whether relating character, plot, setting or theme, teaching students to compare and contrast specific story elements prepares them to make more abstract connections in the future.

Time Required 30–40 minutes

Objectives

- The students will review the definitions for the terms compare and contrast.

- The students will observe how a Venn diagram is used to organize information.

- The students will write a Contrast Couplet poem.

Materials

- visuals from pages 72 and 73

- activity from page 74

- transparency marker

- markers and/or colored pencils for illustrating poems

Procedure

1. Introduce the lesson by displaying the visual from page 72. Read the definition of compare and contrast to the students and explain that they will do an activity that visually demonstrates the concepts of likes and differences using a Venn diagram.

2. Define a Venn diagram as a drawing using overlapping circles to show the relationships between groups of items.

3. Solicit student responses to the question: "What are some things you know about centipedes?" Record these on the transparency. When five to ten characteristics have been recorded, ask the same question about earthworms.

4. Transfer the responses on the list to the correct section of the Venn diagram. Explain that the items listed in the overlapping section are the ways in which centipedes and earthworms compare. The items in the singular parts of the circle are how the two contrast, or are different.

5. Display the visual from page 73 and discuss how the diagram displayed compares and contrasts to the one just created.

6. Inform the students that they are now going to do a creative activity using compare and contrast skills. Give each student a copy of the activity.

7. Read the directions to the students.

8. Ask the students if there are any questions, then allow them the freedom to work together. It is also helpful if they are allowed to look in dictionaries and encyclopedias if they need inspiration for a unique and strange animal to write about.

9. Encourage the students to write more than one poem.

10. Have the students share their poems.

Evaluation

The questions asked on the bottom of the visual should reveal the level of student understanding. If the students are able to note that the questions "How is this diagram similar to the one you created?" and "How is it different?" deal with compare and contrast, they have mastered the concept.

Extension

Students may be curious about the word "couplet." Explain to them that in poetry the number of lines a "stanza" contains has a specific name. (A stanza is a division in a poem or song.) Encourage students to write longer poems about creepy creatures.

Couplet	two-line stanza
Triplet	three-line stanza
Quatrain	four-line stanza
Sestet	six-line stanza
Septet	seven-line stanza
Octave	eight-line stanza

Venn Diagram
Centipedes and Earthworms

Compare—to show how things are similar to one another
Contrast—to show things are different from each other

Class Activity

<u>**Facts about centipedes**</u>   <u>**Facts about earthworms**</u>

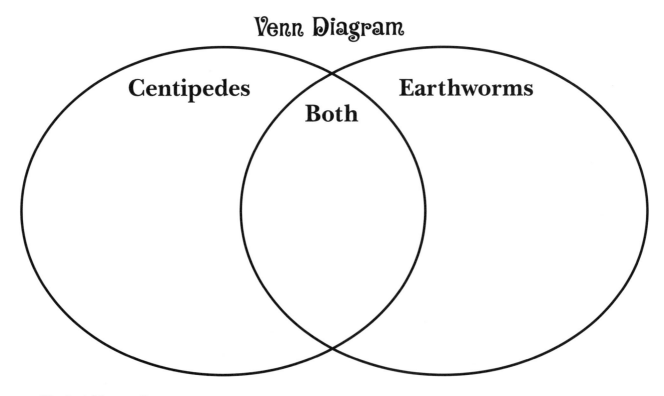

Venn Diagram

Centipedes   Both   Earthworms

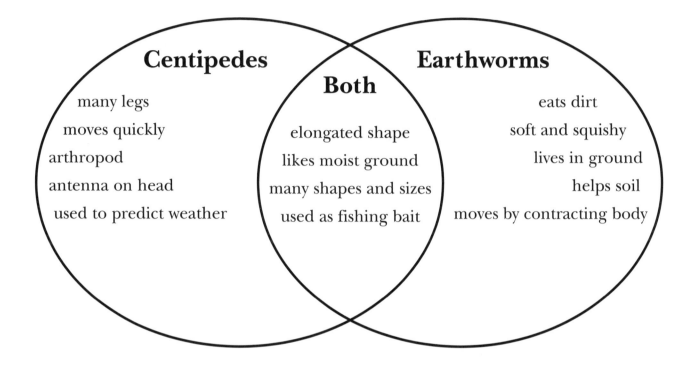

Venn Diagram
Sample
(As created by a group of sixth grade students.)

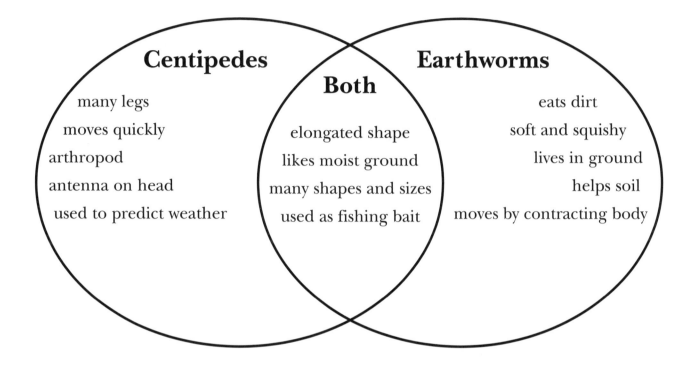

Centipedes
- many legs
- moves quickly
- arthropod
- antenna on head
- used to predict weather

Both
- elongated shape
- likes moist ground
- many shapes and sizes
- used as fishing bait

Earthworms
- eats dirt
- soft and squishy
- lives in ground
- helps soil
- moves by contracting body

How is this diagram similar to the one you created?

How is it different?

Which one do you like better?

Creepy Creature Contrast Couplet

Directions: A couplet is a poem with two lines. Write a couplet that meets the following criteria:

* **The first line includes contrasting words.** These are words that show difference. In the first example below, *thin* and *fat* are the contrasting words.

* **The second line comments on the first line.** The second line is a statement that ties the contrasting words of the first line together. It should rhyme with the first line.

* The topic of your poem should be about a "creepy creature" either real or imaginary.

* You may wish to illustrate your poem.

Examples:

Aunt Spike was brittle and thin while Aunt Sponge was floppy and fat.
It did not matter what their size, the peach did roll them flat.

The centipede has many legs, the earthworm has not a one.
If the two were to have a race, we know who would have won.

Sharp Selection
Motivating Book Selection

"The other edge," the old man went on, "is more subtle still. With it you can cut an opening out of this world altogether."
The Subtle Knife

The Subtle Knife

by Philip Pullman

Story Synopsis

Twelve-year-old Will Parry unintentionally discovers another world while attempting to escape from intruders who are searching for letters written by his missing father, explorer John Parry. This world introduces him to young Lyra Belacqua who is on a mission of her own. The two strong children encounter angels, witches, specters and many dangers on their journey of discovery. When Will loses two fingers and is marked as the new bearer of the "subtle knife," it is apparent that destiny has chosen a reluctant hero.

Introduction

Will Parry, while searching for his missing father, becomes the bearer of a magical subtle knife. This knife allows its owner to open windows to other worlds. Books, too, can allow the reader to enter other worlds. These new worlds can offer information, entertainment and escapism.

Time Required 25–30 minutes

Objectives

- The students will choose an unfamiliar book from the library collection.

- The students will make predictions as to the book's content.

- The students will complete a pre- and post-reading activity.

Materials

- visual from page 77

- activity from page 78

- appropriate books from the fiction collection

Procedure

1. Explain to the students that when directed they are to follow the instructions below:

   - Browse through the fiction section.

   - Select a book that looks either interesting or lonely but one they know nothing about. (The very top and bottom shelves are often good places to look for books that have been unread for a while.)

- Make the book selection using the title only. (The title will be the "subtle knife" that opens the window into the book.)

- Do not open the book until the first part of the activity has been completed.

2. Display the visual.

3. Read the visual to the class, discussing the questions that will be asked. Note that the remarks under the questions serve as clarification to what type of answers may be given.

4. Pass out the activity.

5. Remind the students that they must select their book without opening it and release them to browse the fiction section to make their book selection.

6. When students have checked out their books they may return to their seats to quietly make their predictions.

Evaluation

Completed activity sheets may be returned to the library at a specified date for credit, reward or display. If you are working in collaboration with the teacher, the student's finished project may be accounted for in the classroom grade book.

Extension

During the course of this lesson the students may discover some real gems on the shelves of the library that have gone unread for years. Many of these books have dull, unattractive covers. It is now time to reveal to the students the sad truth that sometimes people do "judge a book by its cover."

Recruit the student artists and graphic arts experts to create new book covers for these unattractive, but wonderful books. Set up a Create a Cover Center in the library. (See the activity on page 79 for written directions that may be posted in the center.) Display examples of attractive book covers and supply needed materials such as paper, pencils, markers and rulers.

Sharp Book Selection

Answer the questions **before** you open the book.
(Use the title, book cover and author to help you with your predictions.)

Who will be the main character?
young boy, pretty girl, wise dog, silly clown

What will some qualities of the main character be?
smart, helpful, adventurous, funny

What kind of book will this be?
mystery, fantasy, humorous, adventure

How many chapters are in the book?
How many pages are in the book?
you can't always tell by the thickness of the book

Is the story illustrated?
photographs, drawings, graphics

Will you want to read another book by the same author?
sometimes authors have written only one book

Sharp Book Selection

Directions: Answer the questions in the first scroll **before** you open the book. Answer the questions in the second scroll **after** reading the book. When you finish, write a short evaluation on how well you were able to predict the content of the book you chose.

Before you open the book...

Book Title: _____ Author: _____

- Who will be the main character? _____
- What will some qualities of the main character be? _____
  _____
- What kind of book will this be? _____
- How many chapters are in the book? _____
- How many pages are in the book? _____
- Is the story illustrated? _____
- Will you want to read another book by the same author? _____

After you read the book...

Book Title: _____ Author: _____

- Who was the main character? _____
- What were some qualities of the main character? _____
  _____
- What kind of book was this? _____
- How many chapters were in the book? _____
- How many pages were in the book? _____
- Was the book illustrated? _____
- Do you want to read another book by the same author? _____

"Create a Cover" Center

Directions: Use the materials provided to "dress up" a book that is fun and interesting but has a dull and dingy cover. Include the following information on the cover:

Front
Title

Author

Illustrations

Back
Reviews

Information about the author

Other books written by the author

Your cover should
Be colorful

Be the correct size to cover the book

Reveal something interesting about the story

Other Books by Edward Eager

1954 *Half Magic*

1956 *Knight's Castle*

1957 *Magic by the Lake*

1959 *Magic or Not?*

1961 *The Well-Wishers*

Edward Eager (1911-1964) born in Toledo, Ohio wrote his first children's book in 1951

F
EAG

Seven-Day Magic

by Edward Eager

back   spine   front

Covers that are accepted will be laminated and placed on the book. Will the new cover improve the book's popularity? Check back with the librarian and see!

The Test of Time
The Classics

A classic is a book that has never finished saying what it has to say.
Italo Calvino (1923–1985)

Introduction

Will the works of Brian Jacques, Phillip Pullman and J. K. Rowling stand the test of time and one day be regarded as classic children's literature? Most experts say that without a doubt Martin the Warrior, Will Parry and Harry Potter will join Frodo Baggins, Peter Pan and Alice of Wonderland as characters in the "must reads" of the future. Giving credit where credit is due, the works of these contemporary authors have proven to motivate reading in both the young and old. When these books have been read and reread, the students are often at the circulation desk asking for another book "just like this one." This is the opportune time to expose eager students to titles that may not have been recently written, but are wonderful literature and exciting to read.

Time Required 25–30 minutes

Objectives

- The students will discuss previously read literature.

- The students will review and recommend a book.

- The students will create an interesting bookmark.

Materials

- visual from page 82

- activity from page 83

- paper

- pencils

Procedure

1. Ask the students why they think some books are so popular while others appeal to a smaller group of people. (Popular books are exciting, scary, easy to read, etc. Books that are "boring" are dated, difficult to read and have dull plots and characters.)

2. Inform the students that most people who like to read about the escapades of the myopic young magician or the valor of a warrior mouse, do so because they like the story's plot, characters or fantastic adventures. Inform the students that when a book is read with enjoyment for several generations it is referred to as "classic literature."

3. Display the visual. Ask the students if any of these titles are familiar to them. Make note that the list is divided into three sections. One section contains books that have a similar plot. The next group of titles deals with the appeal of a misfit or lonely character that overcomes hardships to become a hero. The last section lists fun fantasy books.

4. Allow the students time to check out books or have some of these titles available.

   Note: The books listed are suggestions. A similar list may be created for titles available in the library's collection.

5. Give each student a copy of the activity. Instruct them that reading and reviewing their book, as well as decorating a bookmark that reflects the book's content, is a long-term activity.

Evaluation

Work in collaboration with the classroom teacher concerning a timetable for the completion of the activity. (Completed reviews and decorated bookmarks may also be used as a component of a Reading Month competition.) Completed reviews and decorated bookmarks may be displayed in the library.

Extension

Encourage the students to recommend book titles that others who enjoy the works of Jacques, Pullman and Rowling books might like to read. These book titles could be shared by displaying them on a bulletin board or recording them on a database in the library's computer. These titles tend to be more contemporary and could include: K. A. Applegate's Animorphs Series, Eoin Colfer's Artemis Fowl books and Garth Nix's Seventh Tower Series.

Classic Recommendations

~· Plot ·~
Good Defeats Evil

The Chronicles of Narnia series by C. S. Lewis

The Chronicles of Prydain series by Lloyd Alexander

The Dark is Rising series by Susan Cooper

The Hobbit and *The Lord of the Rings* by J. R. R. Tolkien

The Time Machine and *The Invisible Man* by H. G. Wells

The Wizard of Earthsea by Ursula K. LeGuin

The Wizard of Oz by Frank Baum

~· Character ·~
Misfit Becomes Hero

The Door in the Wall by Marguerite De Angeli

Dragonsong and *Dragonsinger* by Anne McCaffrey

James and the Giant Peach and *Matilda* by Roald Dahl

The Once and Future King by T. H. White

Peter Pan by James M. Barrie

The Secret Garden by Frances Hodgson Burnett

Treasure Island by Robert Louis Stevenson

A Wrinkle in Time by Madeleine L'Engle

~· Genre ·~
Fantasy

Alice in Wonderland by Lewis Carroll

Bed-Knob and Broomstick by Mary Norton

Chitty Chitty Bang Bang: The Magical Car by Ian Fleming

Journey to the Center of the Earth by Jules Verne

Mary Poppins by Pamela L. Travers

The Story of Doctor Dolittle by Hugh Lofting

Classic Recommendations

I, _____, recommend you read,

_____

Written by: _____

This book is interesting because:

_____

_____

_____

_____

_____

_____

_____

_____

_____

_____

_____

_____

_____

_____

_____

I give this book a rating of *(circle one)*

★ Fair   ★★ Very Good   ★★★ Excellent

Create a "classic" bookmark here.

Book List

The Adventures of Captain Underpants by Dav Pilkey. Scholastic, 1997.

The Austere Academy by Lemony Snicket. HarperCollins, 2000.

The Bad Beginning by Lemony Snicket. HarperCollins, 1999.

Dealing with Dragons by Patricia C. Wrede. Harcourt, 2002.

Dinotopia: The Land Apart from Time by James Gurney. HarperCollins, 1998.

Harry Potter and the Prisoner of Azkaban by J. K. Rowling. Scholastic, 2001.

Harry Potter and the Sorcerer's Stone by J. K. Rowling. Scholastic, 1998.

The Hobbit, or, There and Back Again by J. R. R. Tolkien. Houghton Mifflin, 2001.

James and the Giant Peach by Roald Dahl. Penguin USA, 1996.

The Lion, the Witch and the Wardrobe by C. S. Lewis. HarperCollins, 1994.

Quidditch Through the Ages by J. K. Rowling. Scholastic, 2001.

Redwall by Brian Jacques. Ace Books, 1998.

The Subtle Knife by Philip Pullman. Ballantine Books, 1999.

Wizard's Hall by Jane Yolen. Harcourt, 1999.

A Wrinkle in Time by Madeleine L'Engle. Bantam Doubleday Dell, 1981.